Tsunami Warning

This book could not exist without the generous people who kindly gave their time and energy to help. First, I would like to thank John Cloud for making me aware of the story and spending countless hours copying documents about the creation of the Tsunami Warning System in NOAA's central library. For their terrific help with understanding the technology or the history, or in giving their criticism of my dummy, I would like to thank Albert E. Theberge Jr., NOAA historian; Harold O. Mofjeld, oceanographer of the Tsunami Research Program; Mickey K. Moss, chief, Pacific Regional Office of NOAA; Bruce Furukawa of the U.S. Geological Survey; Bruce Turner, geophysicist at the West Coast & Alaska Tsunami Warning Center; Delores Clark, NOAA public affairs officer; Marilyn Ramos of the Pacific Tsunami Warning Center; Jeanne Branch Johnston, earthquake and tsunami program planner of Hawaiian Civil Defense; Brian S. Yanagi, deputy director, and Linda Sjogren, technical information specialist, of the International Tsunami Information Center; Kaleialoha Lum-Ho, archivist of the Pacific Tsunami Museum; Dr. Walter C. Dudley, professor of oceanography at the University of Hawaii at Hilo and director of Kalakaua Marine Education Center; and Rick McKenzie of the Berkeley Seismological Lab. Thanks also go to Kristen Henderson, who modeled as Marsue McGinnis and contributed her unique perspective to the illustrations with the artistic eye of a photojournalist. Lastly, thank you to my friends at Cornelius Elementary School, who let me sketch their schoolchildren pretending to run away from a tsunami.

www.houghtonmifflinbooks.com

Library of Congress Cataloging-in-Publication Data

Morrison, Taylor.
  Tsunami warning / Taylor Morrison.
    p. cm.
  Includes bibliographical references.
  ISBN-13: 978-0-618-73463-4
  ISBN-10: 0-618-73463-5
  1. Tsunami Warning System--History. I. Title.
  GC223.M67 2007
  551.46'370287--dc22

                                        2006035640

Manufactured in China
SCP 10 9 8 7 6 5 4 3 2 1

Tsunami Warning

Taylor Morrison

HOUGHTON MIFFLIN COMPANY BOSTON 2007

Walter Lorraine Books

On December 26, 2004, tsunamis in the Indian Ocean shocked the world. In some places the waves reached heights of more than one hundred feet. After the last wave of the tsunami washed back into the sea, more than 230,000 people had lost their lives. The tragic event motivated governments worldwide to set up their own warning centers.

Now a tsunami warning center in Hawaii watches the Pacific Ocean, the Caribbean Sea, and the Indian Ocean. A warning center in Alaska stands guard over the coasts of the continental United States, Canada, and Alaska. The warning system is based on one invented by a U.S. government agency called the National Oceanic and Atmospheric Association, or NOAA. How did they create it?

The Honolulu Magnetic Observatory at Ewa Beach in 1902

Back in 1925, NOAA was called the Coast and Geodetic Survey, which created a network of magnetic observatories throughout North America. Those working for the survey made maps of the earth's magnetic field so ship captains and surveyors could know the difference between true north and magnetic north on their compasses. The survey's sensitive magnetic instruments began recording an unusual disturbance—vibrations from earthquakes! Instruments called seismographs that record the earth's vibrations were soon installed in the magnetic observatories to start monitoring earthquakes.

At the time, scientists were developing two revolutionary theories. The first was continental drift, or what we call plate tectonics today, the idea that a thin outer shell surrounds the earth and fits together like giant puzzle pieces, and when the pieces slip past one another an earthquake is created. Many American scientists thought this idea was ridiculous. The second theory was that undersea earthquakes and tsunamis were connected somehow. Still, the U.S. government wasn't motivated to create a tsunami warning system until twenty years later, when an earthquake rumbled 12,000 feet below the ocean surface, near a deep canyon called the Aleutian trench.

Thomas Jaggar

As early as 1912 a scientist named Thomas Jaggar began predicting when tsunamis would strike Hawaii after earthquakes occurred. Jaggar worked with the survey to install a tide gauge at Honolulu to monitor tsunamis.

Coast and Geodetic
Survey emblem

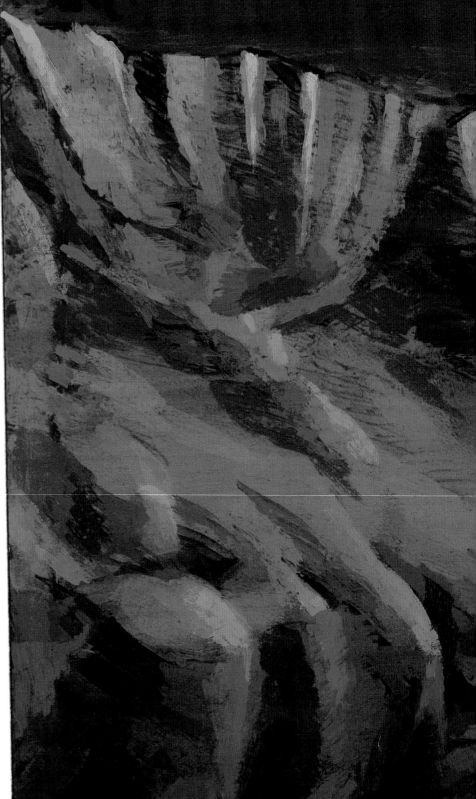

On April 1, 1946, an earthquake violently shook the ground in the Aleutian Islands off the coast of Alaska. Waves spread out from the epicenter toward Unimak Island, eighty miles to the northwest. At two a.m., a giant hundred-foot wave rose above Scotch Cap Lighthouse on the island. The Coast Guard men stationed on higher ground heard the crash of bursting concrete in the early-morning darkness. When the sun rose, the men looked down from the cliffs and were horrified to see that the lighthouse and its five-man crew were washed away. Coast Guard and military men in planes and ships searched the ocean after hearing reports of giant waves, but they could find none.

Unimak Island

Aleutian Islands

Alaska

Hawaiian Islands

The tsunami waves traveled about five hundred miles an hour across the open ocean until they reached Hawaii, 2,300 miles away. Early in the morning the storekeepers, fishermen, and children of Hilo Bay witnessed a bizarre sight. The huge bay was dried up! Men who worked on the docks loading sugar ran into the bay to grab the stranded fish flopping around. Soon a white line of frothing water came into view, and a distant roar announced the arrival of the tsunami.

Hilo Bay

The roar grew louder and louder until it sounded like a hundred freight trains. A terrifying wall of water moved in fast, growing larger and larger. It was as if the land had suddenly sunk below the ocean and the water was rushing in. Many Hawaiians didn't believe the warnings about giant waves because it was April Fool's Day.

The powerful bore lifted the buildings and the railroad depot on the ocean side of Kamehameha Avenue from their foundations and slammed them into the other side of the street with a loud CRASH! The waves tossed around cars, huge boulders, chunks of coral, and railroad cars like toys.

In the open ocean, tsunami waves are hundreds of miles long. They are also very low, so sailors on ships can't detect the subtle rise in the sea. When they approach land, the long, fast-moving waves slow down and concentrate their energy, rising to great heights.

The Coast and Geodetic Survey's seismograph reader, Lieutenant Commander Robert Patterson, was having breakfast when the tsunami hit. Foaming water rushed into his house. Patterson struggled to save the lives of his family as their furniture washed out to sea.

A schoolteacher named Marsue McGinnis watched the first two big waves from inside a cottage at a school on Laupahoehoe Point. The third wave shocked her as it continued to advance and then hit the cottage, breaking all the windows and sucking the building out to sea. She clung to the roof until the powerful currents pulled her underwater again and again. Numb and exhausted, she found a log to cling to. Later on, a U.S. Air Force plane dropped a rubber raft for her. After she had spent nine hours at sea, men in a motorboat rescued her and two boys.

People were desperate to escape the waves. They climbed up trees and onto the roofs of houses, and grabbed on to anything that would float. A six-year-old girl named Jeanne Johnston and her little brother, David, escaped through the jungle behind their home, following a path their uncle Rod cleared by cutting through the thorny vines with a machete.

The tsunami flattened coconut trees and sugar cane fields and spun houses around in the flood. Above the screams the water created a loud sucking sound as each wave washed back out to sea—the most powerful undertow imaginable.

An eerie silence hung over Hilo after the tsunami. The town was strewn with wreckage and body parts. Survivors wore shocked expressions. Railroad bridges were tossed upstream, and a section of railroad track was even wrapped around a tree.

Military personnel carried injured people to get medical treatment, while others pulled victims out of their collapsed homes. Homeless children and families were kept in the barracks at the Hilo Naval Air Station. The Red Cross set up shelters shortly afterward.

"Tidal Wave Death Toll Rises, Loss in Millions," announced the *Washington Post*. Hawaiians were outraged that no one gave them a warning. The waves had claimed 159 lives and caused $25 million in damage. The public and the military both turned their anger on the Coast and Geodetic Survey, because it operated a seismograph that was supposed to detect tsunamis. A navy admiral and an army general lashed out at Lieutenant Commander Patterson, blaming him for not spreading the alarm. Patterson became more aggravated as he repeated his explanation. His seismograph recorded the earthquake onto photographic paper that took a day to develop, so there was no way to read the seismogram until after the tsunami had arrived. "Why don't you fix your machine so it'll ring a bell!" an officer yelled at him.

After the tense meeting, Patterson wrote an angry letter to his boss in Washington, D.C., Commander Elliot Roberts. Roberts was the survey's new chief of geophysics. The shock of the tsunami finally motivated Congress to give Roberts the funding he needed to develop a warning system. The survey had to come up with some innovations in a hurry.

The C&GS's headquarters were in the Commerce Building in 1946.

Commander Elliot Roberts

19

1. Seismic Stations:

Sitka, Alaska

Haviland Hall at Berkeley

Tuscon, Arizona

Over the next couple of years, Commander Roberts organized a massive collaborative effort of the Coast and Geodetic Survey, ingenious scientists, and even the Pentagon, which helped organize an emergency communication system. The Seismic Sea Wave Warning System was operational by 1948. It was quietly successful, but it didn't have a major test for nine years. Then, on March 9, 1957, a powerful earthquake sent shock waves to seismic stations around the world.

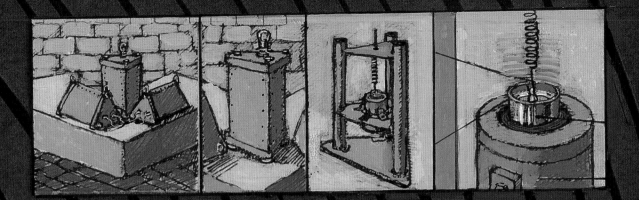

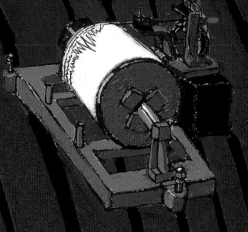

2. Inside the stations, seismometers picked up the earth's vibrations through concrete piers sunk into bedrock.

3. The frame of the seismometer shook with the earth, while a magnet suspended by a spring stayed relatively still.

4. A coil of copper wire on the frame jiggled past the magnet, creating an electric current that went to a seismograph.

5. The stronger the ground motion, the stronger the electric current, which creates a very jagged line drawn on the recording drum.

At 4:30 a.m. in Honolulu, alarm bells rang in the homes of the survey's men on duty. The men jumped out of bed, threw on shoes and pants, and ran to the observatory.

The earthquake registered 8.3 on the Richter scale, big enough to create a large tsunami. Now the scientists had to find out if the earthquake was underwater and could create waves. The central station in Honolulu contacted seismic stations surrounding the Pacific to gather information. How did they find the earthquake in the vast Pacific Ocean basin from squiggly lines on a seismogram?

1. The lines on the seismogram show when different types of earthquake shock waves arrive at a station. P waves travel faster than S waves.

2. The difference in time that P and S waves arrive at a seismic station reveal the distance from the station to the earthquake.

3. Circles around the stations represent distance. The earthquake is found through triangulation, because there is only one place where the three circles could intersect.

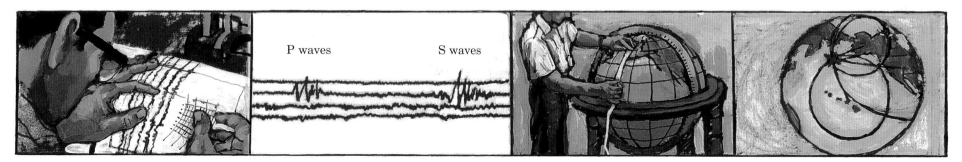

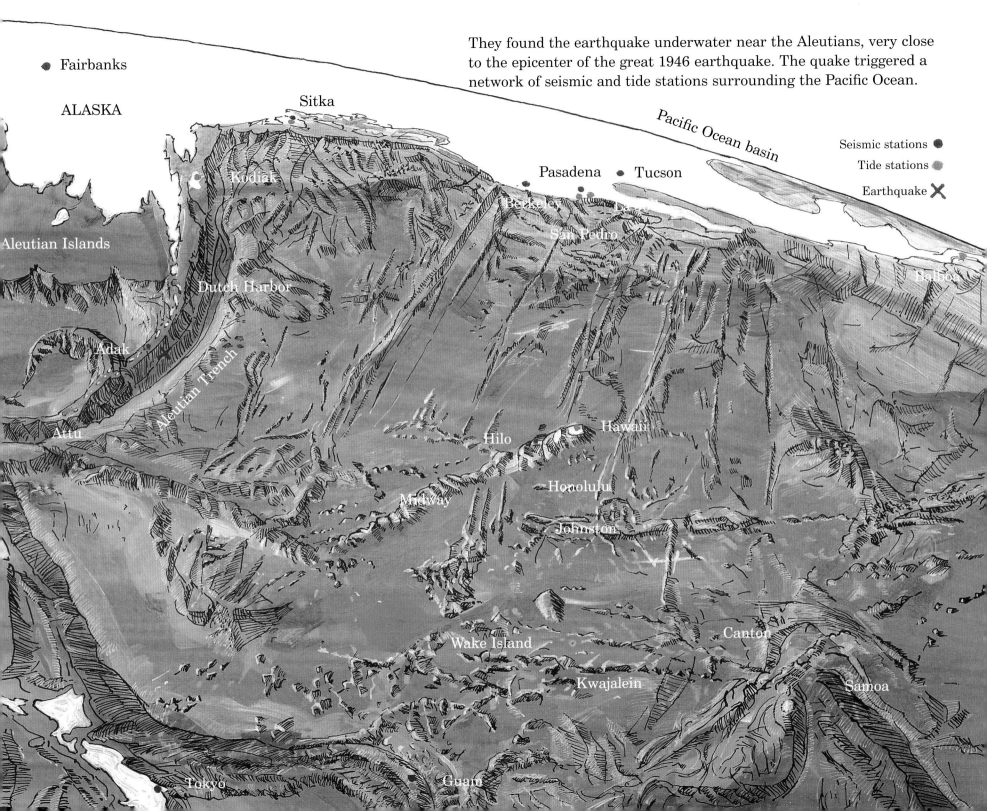

They found the earthquake underwater near the Aleutians, very close to the epicenter of the great 1946 earthquake. The quake triggered a network of seismic and tide stations surrounding the Pacific Ocean.

Pacific Ocean basin

Seismic stations ●
Tide stations ●
Earthquake ✕

Fairbanks

ALASKA

Sitka

Pasadena   Tucson

Berkeley

San Pedro

Kodiak

Aleutian Islands

Balboa

Dutch Harbor

Adak

Aleutian Trench

Attu

Hilo   Hawaii

Midway   Honolulu

Johnston

Wake Island   Canton

Kwajalein   Samoa

Tokyo   Guam

Undersea earthquakes do not always create tsunamis, and false alarms are extremely costly. "Someone's head would be on a platter if ships were sent out to sea and people evacuated to higher ground, and then no big waves arrived," predicted a former tide observer. Small, inconspicuous shacks around the Pacific called tide stations housed tsunami-detecting equipment. Various gauges set off alarms when they recorded the unusually drastic rise and fall of water created by a tsunami. This time, the alarms sent a tide observer running to the end of the dock to check the gauges, risking being hit by an enormous wave. Next an emergency call went out to the police and military. Later that morning, Hawaiians were in a panic. Police ordered people away from the water, sirens wailed, planes took off, people ran uphill, leaving their homes, and ships were sent out to sea.

The unusual rise and fall of water would change the air pressure in the tsunami detector. A tsunami wave would make mercury in a tube rise high or fall low enough to hit electrical connections, triggering an alarm.

Commander Charles K. Green invented a vital part of the warning system that detected long-wavelength tsunami waves.

Inside a tide station, the pencil on a tide gauge recorded the regular rhythm of harbor and wind waves. The gauge drew a very jagged line when it recorded the water drastically rising and falling, as it would with tsunami waves.

24

At about nine in the morning, enormous waves began pounding the shores of Hawaii. The waves caused $3 million worth of damage, but no lives were lost and all the ships were safe.

The exhausted scientists at the observatory were relieved to hear the good news. The commander of all the U.S. Naval forces in the Pacific congratulated Elliot Roberts, who was now a captain. Roberts was happy that all the years of hard work they had put into the warning system were finally recognized.

3. The buoy then sends the data to a satellite, which sends it to warning centers.

2. The data is sent by sound waves thousands of meters to the buoy on the surface.

1. A bottom pressure recorder, or BPR, detects the increased water pressure from a passing tsunami.

"Tsunamis can't be stopped, only understood," said an expert at NOAA. In the past fifty years, scientists have made great leaps in understanding tsunamis. Today much more precise information about a tsunami on the move can be gathered and transmitted to warning centers almost instantly. A new part of the warning system called DART II collects information in the open ocean. Fifteen thousand feet below the sea, instruments can measure the change in water pressure caused by a passing tsunami within a fraction of a millimeter. This "real time" information is sent to a surface buoy, which sends it to a satellite, which in turn relays it to warning centers. Greater knowledge of the landscape below the Pacific Ocean has led to the creation of computer models that can predict where and how fast tsunamis will travel. The models can also determine how large a tsunami will be, just as the models of hurricanes and wildfires predict their paths and intensity. The goals are to decrease false alarms and to react with greater speed and accuracy to real threats.

A tsunami pressure gauge measures changes in water pressure and then transmits this information to satellites.

Pressure sensor

Tsunamis are described as the perfect killer. They don't have a season like hurricanes or tornados do and can arrive unexpectedly, at any time. Shaking ground, an exposed sea floor, and a loud roar are natural warnings.

Today the tsunami warning system in the Pacific is being expanded globally to keep people living in coastal communities safe. The new systems all stand on the foundation of the original ideas, innovations, and hard work of the Coast and Geodetic Survey.

GLOSSARY

ALEUTIAN ISLANDS—A chain of volcanic islands that extends more than nine hundred miles westward from the tip of the Alaskan Peninsula.

ALEUTIAN TRENCH—A long, deep trough under the sea south of the Aleutian Islands where the Pacific Plate descends under the North American Plate.

BORE—The front of a tsunami, which often appears as a flood with a high, abrupt front when it approaches shallow water.

COAST AND GEODETIC SURVEY—A scientific agency responsible for mapping America's coastlines. It was formerly known as the Coast Survey until 1878, and then became a part of NOAA in 1970.

COMMANDER CHARLES K. GREEN—The chief of the Coast and Geodetic Survey's division of Tides and Currents in 1946. He invented a system to detect long-wavelength waves created by tsunamis. It was installed into tide stations and was the heart of the warning system.

DART II (Deep Ocean Assessment and Reporting of Tsunamis)—A system designed to quickly detect and report tsunamis in the open ocean, first tested in the summer of 1995.

EARTHQUAKE—Violent vibrations of the earth caused by the passage of seismic waves radiating from a fault that has suddenly moved.

EPICENTER—The point on the earth's surface directly above an earthquake.

HILO, HAWAII—A town on the northeast coast of Hawaii. Hilo has been hit repeatedly by tsunamis, which are amplified by the wide, shallow bay.

HONOLULU MAGNETIC AND SEISMIC OBSERVATORY—One of many observatories used to map the earth's magnetic field since 1900. Seismographs were used to monitor vibrational disturbances on the magnetic instruments and then used to detect earthquakes.

JAGGAR, DR. THOMAS (1871–1953)—A pioneering geologist who established the Hawaiian Volcano Observatory in 1909. One of Jaggar's main goals was to learn how to predict earthquakes and volcanoes in order to protect people.

NOAA (National Oceanic and Atmospheric Administration)—A government agency that gathers and publishes information about the ocean, coasts, and atmosphere so society can better understand and manage them. Formed in 1970, NOAA includes many agencies, such as the Bureau of Commercial Fisheries and the National Ocean Service. In 1965, the Weather Service took over operation of the Pacific Tsunami Warning Center in Ewa.

PENTAGON—The U.S. military headquarters of the Department of Defense.

RICHTER SCALE—A magnitude scale in common use for rating earthquake energy.

SEISMIC STATIONS—Observatories used to investigate earthquakes. They are in quiet, isolated places, so the instruments are not disturbed by foreign vibrations.

SEISMOGRAM—A physical record of earthquake waves.

SEISMOGRAPH—A recorder that draws, burns, or scratches the vibrations of earthquakes onto rolls of paper from electric signals sent from a seismometer. The seismographs at Ewa in 1957 may have been develocorders, which are like projectors that create a photo-graphic record, or heliocorders, which burn a record into special paper with a hot needle.

SEISMOLOGY—The science of studying earthquakes.

SEISMOMETER—A detector that transforms vibrations of earthquake waves into electric currents. My best estimate of the seismometer used in 1957 is the HVO-2 on display at the USGS Hawaiian Volcano Observatory.

TIDE STATION—A place where tide observations are made.

TSUNAMI—A series of extremely long waves generated by disturbances like earthquakes, landslides, or volcanic eruptions in or near the ocean. The word *tsunami* is a Japanese term meaning "wave in a harbor."

TSUNAMI WARNING CENTER—A place that issues timely information about tsunamis.

Bibliography

Much of my research material came from original documents in the NOAA libraries in Silver Spring, Maryland, and Seattle, Washington.

Bolt, Bruce. *Earthquakes: A Primer.* San Francisco: W. H. Freeman and Company, 1978.

Dudley, Walter C. *Tsunami!* Honolulu: University of Hawaii Press, 1998.

Roberts, Elliot. *Deep Sea, High Mountain.* Toronto: Little, Brown and Company, 1961.

———. *Our Quaking Earth.* Toronto: Little, Brown and Company, 1963.

Walter, C., Dudley Stone, and C. S. Scott. *The Tsunami of 1946 and 1960 and the Devastation of Hilo Town.* Virginia Beach, Va.: Donning Company Publisher, 2000.